CHAPTERS ⚓ HISTORY

Did Columbus Really Discover America?

And Other Questions About the Age of Exploration

by Peter and Connie Roop

■SCHOLASTIC

For Cynthia, our English Mum, who encouraged us
to explore Great Britain!
—C. R. and P. R.

ISBN-13: 978-0-545-07071-3
ISBN-10: 0-545-07071-6

12 11 10 9 8 7 6   12 13/0

Printed in the U.S.A.
First printing, September 2008

Contents

CHAPTER 1

Was Columbus the First European to Come to America?

Many people believe that Christopher Columbus was the first European to come to America. But five hundred years before Columbus first set out in a sailboat, Viking explorers reached America. The Vikings sailed

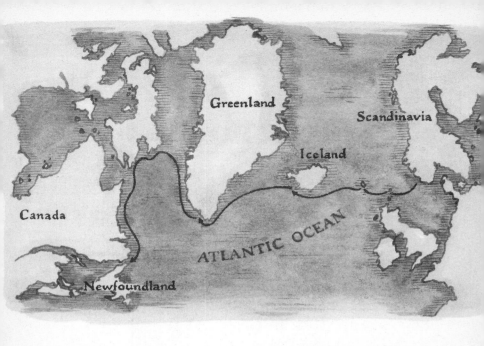

to Iceland and then to Greenland and North America. And like Columbus, the Vikings met the Native Americans, who had already been in America for thousands of years.

The Vikings

The Vikings were explorers and warriors who lived in Scandinavia over a thousand years ago. They sailed strong, fast wooden boats called knarrs. Knarrs were big enough to carry forty people, as well as cattle, sheep, tools, and supplies. Traveling in their knarrs, the Vikings raided other countries.

FACT

The Vikings were also called Norse.

They traded with other countries. And they explored and settled in new lands like Iceland and Greenland.

Lucky Leif

A Viking named Leif Eriksson heard stories about the travels of Bjarni Herjolfsson. Bjarni had discovered a mysterious island on his way to Greenland. Leif planned an expedition to find out what this new land was like.

Thirty-five brave sailors joined Leif when he set sail in 1001. They found Bjarni's flat island. Leif named it Helluland. Leif decided to keep exploring and continued sailing west. The next place they landed was covered with trees. Leif named this Markland.

And still Leif kept sailing. The next place they landed had vines. Leif named this Vinland or Vineland. Today we call it Newfoundland, Canada. Leif and his men became the first Europeans to land in North America! After that, Leif was nicknamed Leif the Lucky because of his lucky discovery.

A Viking Village

Viking men and women followed Leif. They settled in Newfoundland in a place we call L'Anse aux Meadows. They built houses. They raised animals. They fished and hunted. They made the first iron tools in America. But after a few years, the Vikings mysteriously left Canada.

Almost five hundred years would pass before another European, Christopher Columbus, would sail to America.

CHAPTER 2

Did Columbus Think the Earth Was Flat?

Before Columbus began his voyages across the ocean, most people believed that the earth was flat. They thought that a ship that sailed too far would fall right off the end of the ocean. But Christopher Columbus believed the earth was as round as an orange. How did he know the earth was round? Columbus learned that if he watched a ship sailing toward land he would see the top of the ship's mast first. Next he would see the sails. Finally he would see the whole ship. He understood that this could only happen if the earth was round.

Columbus Dreams

Christopher Columbus dreamed he could sail west to reach places like India, China, Japan, and the Spice Islands on the other side of the world.

These places were known as the Indies. Columbus wanted to sail to the Indies to bring back riches such as gold, silver, jewels, silk, pepper, nutmeg, and cinnamon.

Marco Polo's Book

One of Columbus's favorite books was written by Marco Polo. Marco Polo traveled over land to China in 1286. Marco Polo lived in China for twenty-one years. When he came back to Europe, Marco Polo wrote a book about his adventures.

FACT

Marco Polo's book was called *The Travels of Marco Polo.*

Marco Polo wrote about the wonders he had seen. He wrote about the riches of China and Japan. But he also wrote about the dangers of traveling over land. There were tall mountains and wide deserts to cross. There were fierce robbers. There were terrible storms and wars.

Columbus Is Wrong

Christopher Columbus wanted to explore the Indies, but he thought it would be safer to sail to the Indies than to go across land. Since he knew the earth was round, Columbus thought he could sail west around the earth to the Indies.

But Columbus did not know how long it would take to sail across the ocean. And he did not know that North and South America would get in his way.

Columbus Does Not Give Up

Before he could begin his voyage, Columbus needed money and ships. Columbus asked Queen Isabella of Spain to help him. She said no. Still, Columbus didn't give up. He asked the rulers of Portugal, England, and France to help. They all said no. In 1492 he went back to Queen Isabella to ask for help.

And once again, Queen Isabella said no.

Columbus sadly went home. Suddenly, a messenger rode after him. Queen Isabella had changed her mind. She would help Columbus! Christopher Columbus could begin his voyage west in search of the Indies.

CHAPTER 3

Who Sailed With Columbus?

With the money from Queen Isabella, Columbus went to Palos, Spain, to get three ships ready to sail. The *Santa María* was the biggest ship. Columbus would sail on the *Santa María*. The two other ships were called the *Pinta* and the *Niña*. The *Niña* was the smallest ship, but it was also the fastest.

FACT

The *Santa María* was just a little longer than a school bus.

Columbus's Crew

Columbus needed a large crew. He needed sailors to take care of the sails. He needed carpenters to fix leaks. He needed coopers to make barrels. He needed doctors. He needed teenage boys to help the sailors.

The *Santa María* had a crew of forty men and boys. The *Pinta* had a crew of twenty-six. The *Niña* had a crew of twenty-four.

Columbus and his crew spent three months getting the ships ready to sail. Finally, on August 3, 1492, the *Niña*, the *Pinta*, and the *Santa María* lifted their anchors. Columbus was ready to begin his voyage.

Columbus Offers Prizes

The crews settled into life onboard. They raised and lowered the sails. They ate and slept. They talked and sang songs. They watched the unknown water for signs of land.

They prayed they would return home safely.

Columbus offered a prize to the man or boy who spotted land first. He would give the winner one of his silk jackets. The winner would also get gold from Queen Isabella every year for the rest of his life.

The Crew Is Unhappy

But the voyage took longer than Columbus expected. The crew worried that they would run out of food. They worried that they were lost. They wondered if they would ever see Spain again. They worried that sea monsters would swallow the ships.

On October 7, the men told Columbus that if they didn't find land in three days, they would throw him overboard!

Columbus agreed to sail only three more days before returning home.

Land at Last!

The wind grew stronger. The ships sailed faster. A crew member on the *Niña* looked in the water

and saw a branch with a flower on it. Someone on the *Pinta* saw a sharp stick like a spear. These were signs of land!

At ten o'clock on the night of October 11, Columbus saw a light in the distance. At midnight a sailor shouted, *"Tierra! Tierra!"*

When the sun rose on October 12, 1492, the three ships anchored by an island. Columbus thought he had landed in the Indies.

FACT

Tierra is the Spanish word for land.

CHAPTER 4

Did Columbus Really Discover America?

Columbus did not really discover America. Over 100 million Native Americans had lived in North and South America for thousands of years. You cannot discover a place that is already the home of someone else!

And Columbus never really set foot in North America. He actually landed on islands in the Caribbean Sea.

Columbus Lands in the New World

When Columbus landed, he thought he was in the Indies. But he wasn't. He had landed on an island in the Caribbean.

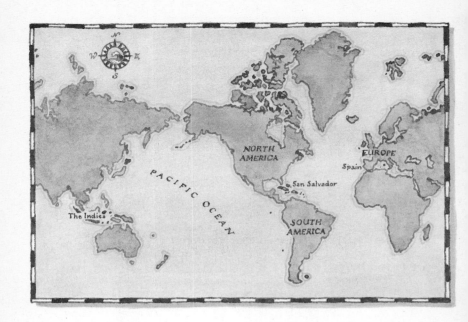

Columbus named the island San Salvador.
He said Spain now owned the island.

Columbus saw people on the island. Since
Columbus thought he was in the Indies, he
called them "Indians."

These "Indians" called themselves Taino.
And they called their island Guanahani.

The Taino People

Long before Columbus arrived, the Taino had been living on Guanahani and other nearby islands, too.

The Taino built houses from palm leaves, wood, and mats woven from reeds. They slept in hammocks they made from cotton rope they spun.

The Tainos were excellent woodcarvers, too. They made spears for hunting lizards, birds, and snakes. They carved wood for spoons and paddles. They made dugout canoes that were large enough to hold forty people!

FACT

Hammocks were a Native American invention. Columbus brought hammocks back to Europe.

FACT

Columbus had never seen a canoe before.

The Taino made fishhooks and harpoons from animal and fish bones. They wove grass to make baskets to carry food.

Columbus thought the Taino were gentle and generous. He was pleased when they traded parrots, cotton thread, spears, and food for the tiny bells, red caps, and shiny glass beads he had brought from Spain.

Columbus Searches for Gold

The Taino wore small pieces of gold jewelry. Columbus was curious about the gold. By making signs with their hands, the Taino told Columbus that the gold came from another island. They told Columbus that the king of that island had a lot of gold.

Columbus thought this rich island must be Japan or even China. He decided to leave San Salvador and keep looking for this other island.

Columbus took six Taino men with him to help him. They guided his ships. They named the islands Columbus passed. Finally they came to a big island the Taino called Colba. Today we call this island Cuba.

Columbus kept searching for the Indies, but he was nowhere near the Indies. After a few months he gave up and sailed home to Spain.

CHAPTER 5

What Was Next for Columbus?

Columbus was greeted like a hero when he returned to Spain in March 1493. After this first voyage, Columbus returned to the

FACT

During all four voyages Columbus never set foot in North America.

New World three more times. He had many adventures and disappointments.

Columbus's Next Voyage

Queen Isabella and King Ferdinand were interested to hear about the people Columbus

met and the places he
saw on his first voyage.
They were pleased with
the gold Columbus
found. Columbus asked if
he could sail again. The
queen and king happily agreed!

Seventeen ships sailed with Columbus
on his second voyage. They sailed in
September 1493.

Columbus explored the New World. But Columbus was having problems. His men treated the Taino like slaves. They made the Taino dig for gold. There were fights between the Spaniards and the Taino.

In March 1496, a disappointed Columbus sailed back to Spain.

Columbus's Third Voyage

Queen Isabella and King Ferdinand wanted more gold. They wondered where the silk, jewels, and spices of the Indies were. They agreed to send Columbus on another voyage, but they said Columbus could sail with only eight ships. Once again, the *Niña* was one of the ships.

FACT

This was the *Niña's* last voyage to the New World.

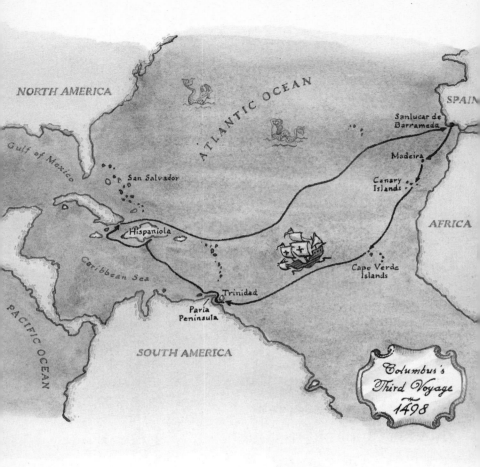

In May 1498, Columbus began his third
voyage. He sailed west and then south.
Columbus's ship landed in South America.

On this voyage, Columbus became the first European to set foot in South America.

The Last Voyage

Columbus's fourth voyage was his last voyage. He sailed in May 1502, with four ships.

Columbus landed on places that would later be known as Honduras, Nicaragua, Costa Rica, and Panama. But the voyage was difficult. His ships survived a hurricane. Columbus got sick. His men got sick. His ship was destroyed in a crash.

Columbus finally gave up. On September 12, 1504, Columbus left the New World for the last time.

CHAPTER 6

How Did America Get Its Name?

If Columbus did not name America, how did it get its name? Columbus thought he had reached the Indies when he landed in the Caribbean. Columbus did not know that he had reached the continents that would become North and South America. The name America came from another explorer, named Amerigo Vespucci.

Amerigo Vespucci

Amerigo Vespucci was born in Italy, just like Christopher Columbus. Vespucci liked to read and do math. He liked to collect maps. He liked to make maps, too. And Amerigo enjoyed thinking about exploring the world.

Vespucci Helps Columbus

In 1492 Amerigo Vespucci was working in a bank in Spain when Queen Isabella gave Columbus permission to go on his voyage. Columbus needed money to prepare his three ships. Vespucci helped Columbus find the money he needed.

Vespucci also helped Columbus get money for his second voyage. When Columbus returned this time, Amerigo Vespucci began dreaming about exploring these new lands himself.

Sailing to the New World

In May 1499, Vespucci sailed on a voyage of his own. Vespucci wanted to make his own discoveries. In less than a month, he reached South America. Vespucci and his men spent many months exploring South America before returning to Spain.

FACT

Vespucci and his men were the first Europeans to see the Amazon River.

Vespucci Sails Again

Amerigo Vespucci sailed to South America again in 1501. He met more native people and wrote about them. He found places no Europeans had seen before. He sailed almost to the end of South America.

Vespucci realized that South America was actually a continent, not part of the Indies like Columbus thought. Vespucci wrote wonderful letters telling everyone about the people he met and the things he saw.

America Gets Its Name

A German mapmaker named Martin Waldseemüller read about Vespucci's discoveries. In 1507 Waldseemüller made a new map of the world. He put Vespucci's findings on his new map.

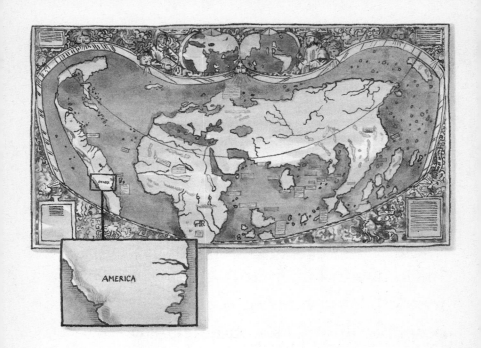

Waldseemüller needed a name for the new land. He called it "America" after Amerigo Vespucci.

CHAPTER 7

Which Explorer Searched for the Fountain of Youth?

Imagine a fountain that has magical water. If you drink the water, you will never be sick and will live forever! Would you explore all over the world for that fountain? People used to believe that there really was a Fountain of Youth. Juan Ponce de León, a Spanish explorer, searched for the mysterious Fountain of Youth for many years. He never found the Fountain, but he became the first European to see Florida and Mexico.

FACT

1,200 men joined Columbus on this voyage.

Ponce de León Sails With Columbus

Juan Ponce de León, a young Spanish soldier, was thrilled to join Columbus on his second voyage. In September 1493, Ponce de León sailed to the New World.

Columbus and his men explored the islands of the New World. They searched for silk, spices, jewels, and gold.

Ponce de León enjoyed these new islands. He saw green rainforests. He watched brightly colored parrots. He met many native people.

The Fabulous Fountain of Youth

One day Native Americans told Ponce de León about the mysterious Fountain of Youth which had magical waters. They told him other Spanish explorers had searched for the fabled Fountain but had never returned.

Ponce de León wondered if they had discovered the Fountain of Youth and were staying near it to drink the water. He decided to search for the Fountain himself.

Finding Florida

Ponce de León explored many islands. He drank water on each island he explored. But none of it was magical.

FACT

Florida means The Flowery Place.

Ponce de León kept sailing. On April 3, 1513, he landed on a flowery shore. He called this place La Florida. Ponce de León became the first European to set foot in Florida.

Landing in Mexico

Ponce de León searched along the whole coast of Florida. He still didn't find the Fountain so he continued to search.

He sailed across the Gulf of Mexico. When he reached land, he again began to look for the Fountain. He didn't find it, but he saw something else. Ponce de León became the first

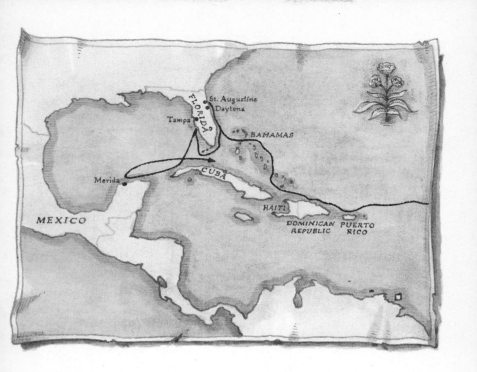

European to set foot in what became Mexico.

Ponce de León had been searching for the Fountain of Youth for many years, without any success. So he finally gave up his search. He didn't live forever, but his story has lived forever because he explored Florida and Mexico, two places no other Europeans had ever seen.

CHAPTER 8

Who Else Explored the New World?

Many other explorers came to the New World after Columbus. Some came from England, France, and Portugal. Many were from Spain. No matter what country these explorers came from, they all sailed to the New World to find fame, wealth, and land. These explorers brought many things to the New World. And they took many New World things back home to Europe.

John Cabot

John Cabot was born in Genoa, Italy, in 1451. After hearing about Columbus's voyages,

Cabot asked King Henry VII of England for permission to explore America. King Henry said Cabot could sail to America under the English flag.

On May 20, 1497, Cabot and eighteen men left England on the *Matthew*. They landed in Canada on June 24. Cabot named the land New Found Land. Many English settlers later followed Cabot to start a new life in Canada.

Ferdinand Magellan

Ferdinand Magellan sailed from Spain in 1519 with five ships. His mission was to find a way past North and South America to reach the Indies.

FACT

Magellan named the Pacific Ocean. *Pacific* means calm.

Pacific
Ocean

SOUTH AMERICA

Atlantic
Ocean

Magellan sailed around the stormy tip of South America and into the calmer Pacific Ocean.

FACT

Magellan died during the return trip, in the Philippine Islands.

In 1522 one of his ships, the *Victoria*, returned to Spain. The *Victoria* was the first ship to sail all the way around the world!

Francisco Coronado

Francisco Coronado was the governor of Mexico. He heard tales of seven golden cities north of Mexico. In 1540 Coronado set out to find the Seven Cities of Gold.

Coronado reached the first city. But he was very disappointed. The city was made of yellow adobe, not gold!

Coronado explored for two long years. He searched as far as Kansas, but never found a single golden city. Some of his men, however, became the first Europeans to see the Grand Canyon!

Hernando de Soto

Hernando de Soto was a Spanish explorer. He had heard that Florida was a land rich in gold. Starting in 1539, de Soto and his men explored for two years. They started in Florida and traveled through what is now known as North Carolina, South Carolina, Georgia,

Alabama, Tennessee, and Mississippi. Many men died from diseases. Others died in battles with Native Americans.

During his search, de Soto reached a wide, muddy river. Today we know this river as the mighty Mississippi. De Soto and his men were the first Europeans to see the Mississippi River.

The Whole World

The New World changed after the other explorers arrived. They brought horses, sheep, pigs, cattle, guns, and iron tools to the Americas. They also brought diseases and violence, which killed many Native Americans. Their world would never be the same.

But the Native Americans changed the Old World, too. Europeans learned about potatoes, tomatoes, corn, turkeys, pumpkins, chocolate, canoes, snowshoes, oranges, and peanuts from the Native Americans. They used this knowledge when they settled in the New World and they brought back information to their countries in Europe.

How would your life be different if Columbus and the other explorers had never left home?